THE HUGE ALLOSAURUS

BY PETER FINN

DINOSAUR WORLD

Enslow PUBLISHING

DISCOVER!

Please visit our website, www.enslow.com. For a free color catalog of all our high-quality books, call toll free 1-800-398-2504 or fax 1-877-980-4454.

Library of Congress Cataloging-in-Publication Data

Names: Finn, Peter, 1978- author.
Title: The huge allosaurus / Peter Finn.
Description: New York : Enslow Publishing, [2022] | Series: Dinosaur world | Includes index.
Identifiers: LCCN 2020049019 (print) | LCCN 2020049020 (ebook) | ISBN 9781978521124 (library binding) | ISBN 9781978521100 (paperback) | ISBN 9781978521117 (set) | ISBN 9781978521131 (ebook)
Subjects: LCSH: Allosaurus–Juvenile literature.
Classification: LCC QE862.S3 F5574 2022 (print) | LCC QE862.S3 (ebook) | DDC 567.912–dc23
LC record available at https://lccn.loc.gov/2020049019
LC ebook record available at https://lccn.loc.gov/2020049020

Published in 2022 by
Enslow Publishing
101 West 23rd Street, Suite #240
New York, NY 10011

Designer: Sarah Liddell
Interior Layout: Rachel Rising
Editor: Therese Shea

Illustrations by Jeffrey Mangiat
Science Consultant: Darla Zelenitsky, Ph.D.,
Assistant Professor of Dinosaur Paleontology at the University of Calgary, Canada

Photo credits: Cover, pp. 1, 5, 7, 9, 11, 13, 15, 17, 19, 21 (rock border) SirinR/Shutterstock.com; pp. 2, 4, 6, 8, 10, 12, 14, 16, 18, 20, 22, 23, 24 (background) altanaka/Shutterstock.com; pp. 5, 7, 15, 19 (egg) fotoslaz/Shutterstock.com.

Portions of this work were originally authored by Nina Theresa and published as *Allosaurus*. All new material this edition authored by Peter Finn.

Printed in the United States of America

CPSIA compliance information: Batch #CSENS22: For further information contact Enslow Publishing, New York, New York, at 1-800-398-2504.

CONTENTS

Boldface words appear in Words to Know.

MEET ALLOSAURUS

Allosaurus was a huge meat-eating dinosaur. It lived more than 144 **million** years ago! This was a time called the Jurassic Period. *Allosaurus* **fossils** tell us what this dinosaur looked like. Fossils also help us imagine how it acted.

HOW TO SAY
ALLOSAURUS:
AL-OH-SORE-US

A BIT DIFFERENT

The first *Allosaurus* fossil was discovered in 1877. *Allosaurus* means "different lizard." *Allosaurus* had backbones unlike other dinosaur fossils that had been found. The backbones were a different shape. They had **hollow** parts. Birds have bones like this too!

DINOSAURS AREN'T LIZARDS. THEY'RE **REPTILES!**

WHERE DID THEY LIVE?

Scientists have found *Allosaurus* fossils in North America, Europe, Africa, and Asia. Most *Allosaurus* fossils have been found in the western United States. In Utah, 46 *Allosaurus* fossils have been uncovered. Even more have been discovered in Colorado and Wyoming.

WHERE *ALLOSAURUS* FOSSILS WERE FOUND

HOW HUGE?

Some *Allosaurus* were 16 feet (5 m) tall. That's taller than *Tyrannosaurus rex*! *Allosaurus* could grow to more than 40 feet (12 m) long too. That's about the length of three small cars. It could weigh more than 4,000 pounds (1,814 kg).

40 FEET (12 M) LONG
16 FEET (5 M) TALL

HEAD TO TAIL

Allosaurus had a large, narrow head. It had **ridges** on its face. It had two small horns above its eyes too. *Allosaurus* arms were short. However, this dinosaur had big, strong back legs. Its long tail helped it **balance**.

LARGE HEAD
LONG TAIL
STRONG LEGS

THEROPOD

Allosaurus was a theropod. Theropods were a group of meat-eating dinosaurs. They were bipedal (by-PEH-dahl). That means they walked on their back legs. All had short arms. They were many sizes. *Tyrannosaurus rex* was a theropod too!

THE NAME THEROPOD MEANS "BEAST FOOT."

PREDATOR!

Allosaurus was a predator. It hunted other animals for food. It had three pointy claws on each hand. It had sharp teeth to tear its **prey** to pieces. These teeth **curved** backward to stop prey from getting away.

CLAWS TO
HOLD PREY

WHAT'S TO EAT?

Allosaurus ate plant-eating dinosaurs. *Allosaurus* hunted *Diplodocus* (dih-PLAH-deh-kuhs) and *Stegosaurus* (steg-uh-SOHR-uhs). These dinosaurs ate plants, but they could fight. *Diplodocus* may have used its big tail to knock over enemies. *Stegosaurus* had a tail with **spikes**!

ALLOSAURUS WAS LIKELY A SCAVENGER TOO. THAT MEANS IT ATE DEAD OR DYING ANIMALS IT FOUND.

NEW DISCOVERY

Scientists think there were several species, or kinds, of *Allosaurus*. In 2020, they reported they found a new species. So far, four species have been found in all. What will scientists discover next about this giant meat-eating dinosaur?

ALLOSAURUS

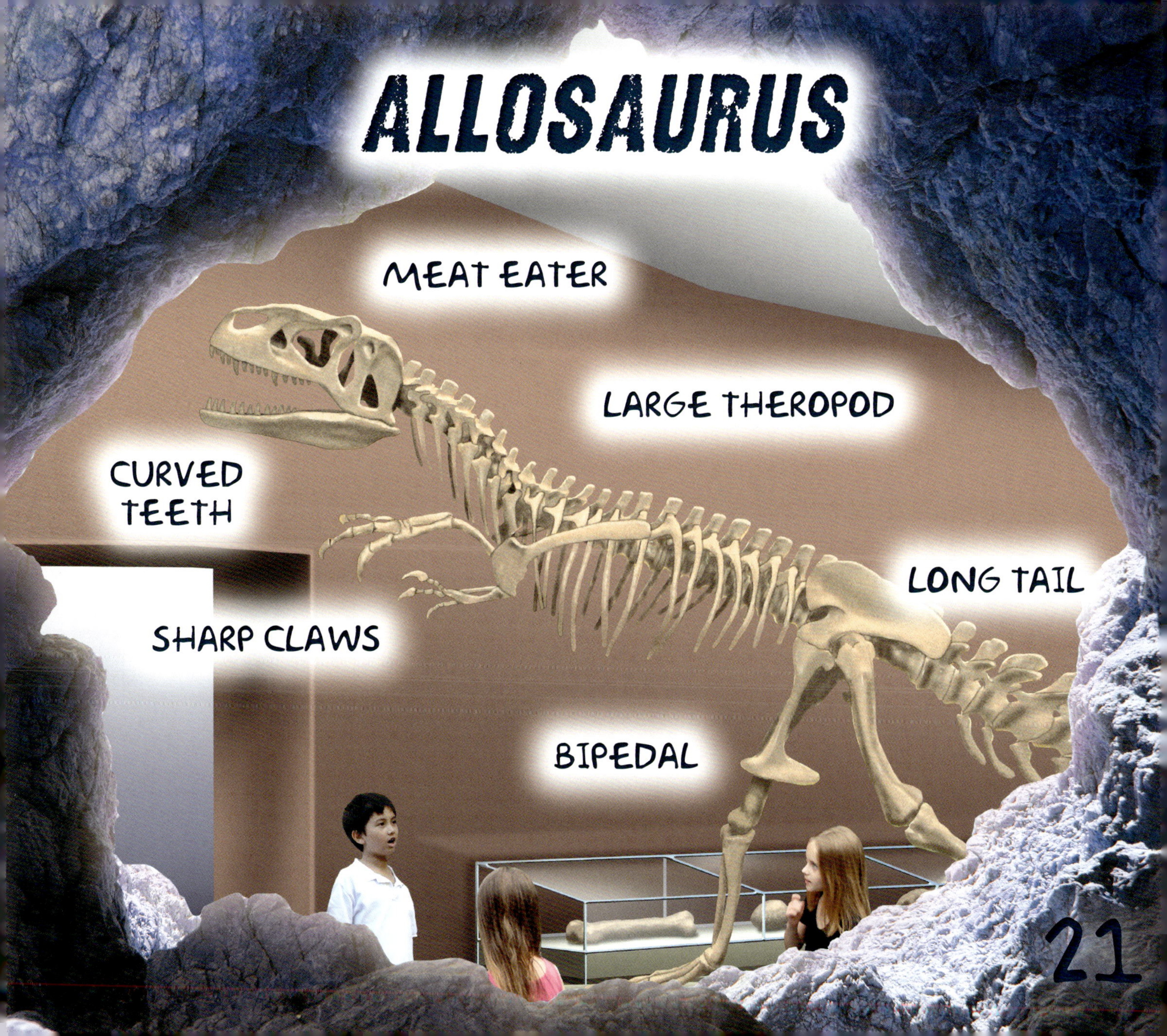
MEAT EATER
LARGE THEROPOD
CURVED TEETH
LONG TAIL
SHARP CLAWS
BIPEDAL

WORDS TO KNOW

balance Being able to stay in place without falling.

curved Rounded.

fossil The hardened marks or remains of plants and animals that formed over thousands or millions of years.

hollow Having nothing inside.

million A thousand thousands, or 1,000,000.

prey An animal hunted by other animals for food.

reptile An animal covered with scales or plates that breathes air, has a backbone, and lays eggs.

ridge A raised area.

spike Something long and thin that ends in a point.

FOR MORE INFORMATION

BOOKS

Bradley, Timothy J. *I Am Allosaurus*. Mt. Pleasant, SC: Arbordale Publishing, 2020.

Ringstad, Arnold. *Allosaurus*. Minneapolis, MN: Cody Koala, 2019.

Sabelko, Rebecca. *Allosaurus*. Minneapolis, MN: Bellwether Media, 2021.

WEBSITES

Allosaurus
www.nhm.ac.uk/discover/dino-directory/allosaurus.html
See how big this dinosaur was compared to a human.

***Allosaurus* Facts for Kids**
www.sciencekids.co.nz/sciencefacts/dinosaurs/allosaurus.html
Read some quick facts about *Allosaurus*.

INDEX